ACCOUNTING: THE SUPER-DUPER FUN PART OF STARTING A BUSINESS

How to Confidently Give Your Business a Solid Foundation

TRESSA HEATH, CPA

Tressa Heath, CPA

ACCOUNTING, THE SUPER DUPER FUN PART OF STARTING A BUSINESS

How to Confidently Give Your Business
a Solid Foundation

TRESSA HEATH, CPA

Tressa Heath, CPA

ISBN-13: 978-1481855273
ISBN-10: 1481855271

Dedication

I dedicate this book to my husband, my family and friends, my loyal clients, and the outstanding business community of Greater Lafayette. Thank you for your unwavering support!

Contents

Accounting: The Super-Duper Fun Part of Starting A Business

Acknowledgements

Every now and again we all need a little encouragement to do something beyond what we think is possible by ourselves. My thanks to Nicole Gebhardt for giving me the courage and the guidance to publish this book.

My Story

On December 13, 2011, I walked into my first day as the owner of Heath CPA & Associates. My very own firm. It was terrifying and exciting all at the same time. I had done my homework. I was taking the steps which need to be taken to start a business.

But...I was still taking a risk. I placed my career and, much more importantly, my family on the line by giving up a steady paycheck to put most of our savings into a startup.

At the time, our kids were 20 months and 8 months old. Not only would this be challenging and risky financially, but the juggle of being a wife, mom, and business owner was another slight concern. (And by the way, I had my third baby before hitting the one-year anniversary of the business. Insanity.)

However, I had done all the preparations I could, and financial projections showed this would be profitable. While it would certainly be more work, it would allow much more flexibility, allowing me to enjoy my family and raise my kids. No one else would dictate when that could happen.

With the support of my husband, family, friends and our outstanding business community, I made the leap and became a business owner. It was the best decision I've ever made.

In some ways, my leap was a bit easier than yours may have been. My diverse career as a CPA gave me varied knowledge about running a business. Clearly, I knew bookkeeping, how to set up my entity, and other "super duper fun" accounting things. Also, similar to being the girl who watches her friends raise kids before having her own and getting the benefit of seeing first-hand what works, what doesn't and what style best fits me, I have also observed my business owner clients over the years, which is an invaluable benefit.

Since that first day of my new firm, I've advised many clients who are starting a business. But now my perspective is different. The experience I offer is different. *I* am the business owner, now. My view is poles apart from that of a CPA with a big firm to "back them up."

It's with this personal experience perspective that I've written this book for you. A bit of it tongue in cheek, but all of it sound advice from a person who's been in your shoes and knows what it takes to start a business with a solid foundation. Let's get started.

The Scoop

Whether you're buying an existing business or starting one from scratch, by the time you're reading this book, hopefully you've already asked and answered the question: **"Should I start/buy this business?"** You've concluded there's a need and market for your product, you can make a profit selling it and you've got what it takes to be a successful business owner, which is probably the most important factor. If you're still in the beginning stages of answering that question, I have included some resources on my website, www.heath-cpa.com, to help you.

Now what?

This can be a very scary time filled with emotion which makes it all very overwhelming. There may be several people giving you advice. It can be hard to weed out the good suggestions from the bad. A good rule of thumb would be: listen to the experts and professionals in any given area. If you have an uncle who owns and runs a successful business, you should absolutely squeeze every ounce of business advice out of him that you can. But unless he's an attorney too, don't listen to any tidbits he thinks he knows about the law. Find an attorney. Or, you have a friend who does his own tax return every year. Unless your friend is also a CPA, that does not mean he's an expert on taxes. Find a good CPA.

I get excited about our business community, and I want every business owner to succeed. Just before starting my firm, Nicole Gebhardt, a marketing coach and founder of TheRemarkableWay.com, gave me some great advice: **a successful business is one that is not only profitable, but is one you love and fits in with your desired lifestyle**. The purpose of this book is to help you gain direction in starting your business with a great foundation that will set it up for success. I'll give you tools, direction, and advice as both a Certified Public Accountant (CPA) and a small business owner who has gone through this possibly painful but definitely exciting process. It's not an easy thing to do. If it were, anyone could do it, as they say.

Chapter 1

Don't be Dumb.
Do it Right.

As I have already said, even if there is a market for your product and it has the potential to make a profit, the factor of whether or not you should be a business owner is the most important piece of the puzzle. Of all of the business owners who come through my door, there are three main common traits I see in the most successful ones.

First, they seek out and utilize resources.

Since you're reading this book, I'm guessing you have this first trait. You are not the first and only person to start a new business. Take advantage of all the resources available for you from people who have been there and done that. That could mean within your own community, global network, or online.

Hopefully you're either located in Lafayette, IN or your community is as supportive as ours. If you don't know where or how to begin looking, start with contacting your local chamber of commerce. In Lafayette, it will point you to the Small Business Development Center and SCORE, which are both FREE resources.

Second, they're more proactive than reactive.

Forming the correct foundation early is vital in building a successful business. The kind of entity you register as dictates how much you pay in taxes. Setting up bookkeeping early and properly not only gives you the information you need to monitor and run your business well. It also makes the ugly task of bookkeeping easier, as things only get more complicated as you grow. If you have partners, having a good operating agreement in place from the start is smart. Opening a separate bank account for your business cuts down on things getting intertwined with your personal account. I could go on and on listing all the reasons you and your business benefit from getting it done right from the start…and I guess I sort of do as I write this book.

Among other things, hire a CPA before you open your doors. (Or if you have already opened when reading this, stop everything and do it now!) There's a big difference in that versus realizing it's almost April 15th in the year after you've started your business and scrambling to find someone capable of doing taxes just to fill the requirement to file.

Third, they are involved in their community and network 'til their feet and jaw are sore.

There are many ways to build your network and, therefore, your business. Your local chamber of commerce is a great place to start for this, also, if you haven't already.

Years ago, I had a boss who mentored me about networking. He stressed the importance of slowly building relationships rather than focusing on seeking out hot leads. I got involved in Greater Lafayette Commerce and Tippy Connect Young Professionals. I attribute most of the business I have to getting involved with those organizations and the relationships I have formed within them over the years. Because of them, when I went out on my own I already had a growing client base and the necessary relationships in and knowledge of our community to efficiently serve my clients and run my firm.

There are a number of other networking groups available in any community, such as Business Networking International (BNI) or Rotary Club. You could join the board of a nonprofit dear to your heart. Just do something other than hanging a sign, building a website and waiting for customers. Go get them!

Tressa Heath, CPA

Chapter 2

Choosing an Accountant You...Love?

Yeah that's right...you should love your accountant! Trust me...it's possible!

The main reason for this chapter is to educate you on how to know if the accountant you're sitting in front of really knows what they're talking about and will give you the service you need and deserve. This can be very tricky because you're probably not an accountant and you don't know what you don't know. When someone claims to know what they're talking about and is a working professional in any field, you often just trust that is the case. If you've never had experience with someone in a certain profession, you may assume the level of service you receive from the first one you come across is standard, even if it's unacceptable.

As I've said already, I love my community and want every business owner to succeed. When I hear of someone using a known substandard accountant, my standard line is as follows, "You don't have to use me as there are plenty of great CPAs in this town, but please don't use that person for another day." There really are many great firms and accountants, but, as in any profession, there are some not great ones. A good accountant can make a big difference to you and your business in several ways.

Here are some things to pay attention to and note when choosing your accountant.

How easy was it to reach them?

We all make mistakes. Messages get misplaced, we take vacation days, we are out of the office, etc. If it takes more than a couple of times calling someone without receiving a prompt call back, this is a sign communication with them will always be poor. A good accountant should focus on communication and accessibility. There will be times you need to contact your accountant immediately. If communication is not there, it will make running your business more difficult than it needs to be.

At your first consultation, do they get to know you and your business before giving you specific advice?

I used to think this was a given, but I've learned recently it's not. No two businesses are the same. There are several variables which play into every decision and piece of advice an accountant gives. The initial consultation should begin with you telling your story including why you are or want to be in business, what your business is, how your family works into your business, your goals both personally and professionally, and other extremely important details like those. If you receive advice before giving any information like that, there is a high probability you are not receiving good advice. At a minimum it probably means you'll leave that initial consult without all of your questions answered and without all of the information you need.

Are you given options?

A while ago I left my longtime dentist because it felt like they stopped caring about me and started wanting to sell me things. Like any profession, your accountant should give you options in services they can provide verses things you can do on your own. This also depends on several things such as your budget, your technical abilities or personnel, your available time, the accounting and tax needs of your business, and often the personality of the business owner. There are definitely a few things your accountant and only your accountant should do but not many. There are several things which make more sense for you or an employee to take care of with an accountant's support, again depending on a number of different variables. You should never feel like you're being sold on something without your needs being considered and some options given to you.

Are they involved in the business community with a good network of professionals and referral partners?

This isn't necessarily a make or break kind of quality. However, there are three reasons why this matters.

First, building your team of professionals to take great care of your business can be tricky. A good accountant is just one piece of the puzzle. We'll talk about this more in Chapter 4, but if your accountant can provide you with a list of professionals they know will provide the level of service you need, building your team is much easier. Their referral partners should be extensions of themselves and people you will also like and trust.

Second, an accountant with a strong network of business professionals will be able to operate more efficiently and with a higher quality of service. For instance, an accountant's bank contacts can make managing your accounts much easier and more accurate. Also, attorneys and accountants commonly need to work together to come up with the best solution for a problem or situation. There are many decisions which crossover into other areas of your business and being able to easily work well with other professionals is important.

Third, if your accountant is involved in and cares about their community, chances are good they'll care about you and your business and they'll be well-rounded with knowledge in several areas.

Are they an expert in their field?

This is a tricky one because, again, you don't know what you don't know. However, we have instincts for a reason and we should listen to them. If you at all question whether or not they really know what they're talking about, find someone else. You might be wrong, but this is a factor of being comfortable with your accountant and working well with them. If you doubt them, right or wrong, it may affect how you take and use their advice.

This doesn't necessarily mean they need to specialize in your specific industry. Especially in cities the size of Lafayette, IN or smaller, it would be rare to find an accountant who specializes in construction companies, for example. You should find one who has *experience* in the construction industry, but it's not necessary to find a specialist. I had a client leave me because I wouldn't claim to specialize in her industry but could only assure her I had plenty of experience in it. She found someone who *did* claim to specialize in her field but she soon returned to me because she quickly discovered her accounting needs didn't warrant complex services and the specialized price that went with it. Remember: being too specialized isn't necessarily a good thing.

Do you love your accountant?

Okay, maybe you don't have to truly love your accountant, but you should like them a lot, find them relatable, and enjoy talking with them. The days of accountants being boring number crunchers with no personality are gone...or they should be anyway! You should be able to find an accountant with all the qualities listed above along with a personality which fits yours. Accounting is painful enough (to most people) without having to discuss it with someone who makes it worse rather than better. It's too important to you and the success of your business to have someone you dread contacting. If their personality, or lack of personality, makes you hesitate to communicate with them it could have a very negative impact on your ability to make good decisions and operate your business properly. We're an important part of helping you succeed!

Chapter 3

What Kind of Entity Should I Be? (Um...what's an entity?)

Well just like you (and your spouse, if applicable) are a taxpaying entity and considered "individuals" in the eyes of the IRS and other related agencies, your business will need to register to be a separate entity. The most common types to choose from are sole proprietor, Limited Liability Company (LLC), S-Corporation, and C-Corporations, and I'll briefly explain each one. However please do not read this and make a determination on your own of which one best fits you. This is a big decision and is the basic framework for your business. You should definitely discuss this with your CPA (not an attorney) as it is impossible for me to cover every aspect of why a particular type of entity may be right for you.

Sole Proprietors

This could only be an option for business owners without partners. The biggest benefit about being a sole proprietor is the low administrative burden and cost. It can be a great entity to start with if you're uncertain about how successful and profitable it's going to be, at least in the short term, because you can switch to a different type of entity easily from a sole proprietorship.

It takes very little work to form. Potentially, you could do nothing and have a sole proprietorship and just start operating.

Administrative costs are low because you have fewer filing fees with various agencies to register your business and you report the income and expenses directly on your individual tax return on a Schedule C. That cuts down on the work (and fees) you'll have to send to your accountant. If you don't have employees, you don't necessarily need payroll so there's no administrative cost or burden there.

However, there are some major reasons which may make the administrative ease of a sole proprietorship less appealing.

First, you don't have any liability protection. It's referred to as the corporate veil and sole proprietors don't have one. An attorney would and should explain this better than me, but basically your business is an extension of you and, therefore, if someone sues your business and all of its assets they can also sue you and all of your personal assets. Some industries are, of course, riskier than others, but you never know what could happen.

Second, if you're making a profit, you could be paying a large self-employment tax on top of the already-hard-to-swallow income tax. If this is the case, you could potentially save money by registering as a different entity. I loosely use a rule of thumb of about $7,500-$12,500 net profit as a guide of when it's time to start talking about different entity options to get rid of that nasty self-employment tax.

Limited Liability Company (LLC)

Single-owner LLCs have similar traits of a sole proprietor. Both are considered "disregarded entities" by the IRS. Therefore, the income and expenses are reported directly on the owner's individual tax return on a Schedule C, which, again, can cause self-employment taxes. However, an LLC keeps administrative costs lower because you have one tax return.

Unlike sole proprietors, you do have a corporate veil of protection in regard to legal liability. That's something very important to consider. Also, you will have some filing fees with the state to register your entity, and you'll need to get an employer identification number and do a few other administrative filings to register your business. If you have one or more partners, you'll be a multi-owner LLC, which is not a disregarded entity. It is, however, a "flow-through entity." This means the entity does not pay taxes. Instead, the tax return the business files is only informational and calculates how much and the type of income each partner should report on their individual tax return.

There are a few reasons and benefits to being a multi-owner LLC.

- As a flow-entity, you can avoid double taxation when you take cash out of the company.

- If you're buying real estate, or other appreciating property, it is recommended you hold that property in an LLC rather than a corporation to avoid the possibility of paying two levels of tax upon the sale and liquidation of the business.

- You have flexibility in an LLC to split the income, expenses, and equity in different ways, if you want or need to.

- There are few limits of who can be a partner in an LLC.

However, a big reason not to be taxed as an LLC is to avoid self-employment tax. The net trade or business income of general partners and guaranteed payments of limited partners are subject to self-employment tax in addition to income tax. If other factors allow for it, avoiding self-employment tax should be a part of the decision of whether to be an LLC or a corporation.

S-Corporations

S-Corporations are, also, flow-through entities. The shareholders report their portion of income on their tax returns, and double taxation is not a factor. There are some big differences between LLCs and S-Corps though.

Whether there is one owner or multiple owners, the S-Corp files an annual income tax return. This is one area where administrative costs can be higher since it is recommended you have a CPA prepare the business tax return in addition to your personal tax return.

Partnerships, corporations, and non-resident aliens are not allowed to be shareholders in S-Corps. With today's global economy this can be a reason not to be an S-Corp if you have non-resident alien shareholders or partners.

Another possible drawback to S-Corps is: all profit, loss and equity must be split according to percentage of ownership. There is no flexibility in this area as with LLCs.

The biggest benefit to being an S-Corp (or electing to be taxed as an S-Corp) is: net income is not subject to self-employment taxes as with LLCs. However, officers (including owners) who perform more than minor services to the business are required to be paid a reasonable wage for their services. Those wages are subject to employment taxes. This is where, as an S-Corp, we gain control over how much you pay in employment taxes each year.

I'll attempt to illustrate: If you were a member of an LLC with $100,000 of net income in a given year, you would pay self-employment taxes (on top of income taxes) on the full $100,000. If this same entity were an S-Corp and the reasonable wage the owner should be paid is only $40,000 annually, that is the only amount subject to employment taxes.

The full $100,000 would still end up being subject to regular income taxes, but you would save employment tax costs on $60,000. That's a *great* amount of money saved, and that savings would certainly make any additional administrative burden and cost worth it!

A great thing about S-Corps is they can start as either C-Corps, which I'll talk briefly about next, or LLCs. You register as one entity and elect to be taxed as an S-Corp either right away or when the circumstances indicate this is the best choice for the business.

C-Corporations

I'm not going to go into much detail about C-Corporations as it is rare a C-Corporation would be a good fit for a small business. The biggest reason is you run into problems with double taxation with C-Corporations…and double taxation is usually bad.

When a C-Corp files a tax return it pays tax at the corporate level. When a shareholder takes a dividend or distributions of those already-taxed profits, that dividend is taxed on the individual's tax return. Double taxation.

Two reasons, in today's tax environment, to be a C-Corporation is if you would like to be publicly traded now or eventually or if you will have more than 100 shareholders.

I cannot stress enough that just reading this book, especially this section, does not mean you should do your own analysis of what kind of entity to register as without the council of a CPA. This is not something most attorneys should advise on either. However, hopefully this basis of knowledge will help you think through your options with your CPA. Get it right from the start!

Tressa Heath, CPA

Chapter 4

Building Your Professional "Posse"

This was another area I benefited from tremendously when I started my firm. I didn't have to waste time shopping around for who I was going to use. Instead, at every step of the process I knew whom to call and they would take excellent care of my business and me. This is why I stressed finding professionals who already have a good network of other professionals to refer. (My posse rocks!)

Depending on the specific factors of how your business will begin and operate, you will need a variety of professionals to help you.

Attorney

An attorney is strongly recommended, but not always necessary. If you do need one, an attorney is one of the first people you seek council from along with a CPA. The two will work together to build the proper foundation for you. I especially recommend using an attorney if you have partners or if you are buying an existing business. Please, do *not* use any do-it-yourself legal products. In some instances I would rather you have no documents at all over legal documents you created yourself.

An attorney (or in many cases, your CPA) will also help you establish the right business entity for your new business.

Banker/Lender

Once you have a registered entity with an employer identification number (EIN), the next step is to get a bank account for the business. The sooner you do this and start paying for all business expenses out of this account, the more likely it is you will not miss deductions when it's time to file your taxes. If you miss deductions, you pay more taxes.

A relationship with a good bank and banker becomes even more important when you have a business account verses just a personal account. There are many more complexities to business accounts and you quickly see that not all banks are the same once you have one. Your bank should offer a variety of products to help small businesses run efficiently and a banker who focuses on customer service.

If you're in need of a loan to buy an existing business, for start-up operating expenses, to buy equipment, etc., I encourage you to shop around and apply at several banks. You won't hear me say that often because I'm decisive and I don't like to waste time shopping. However, in today's lending environment, it is not as easy to get loans as it used to be and the process can take a long time.

I had to get a loan to buy my current firm. I started with two banks, thought one was going to be able to help me, realized they weren't the right fit and picked up the process again with the other bank where I ultimately got approval. The entire process took about 5 months from when I started my inquiries to closing on the purchase of the business.

It wasn't entirely the bank's fault though. I, unfortunately, was dealing with a very difficult seller, too. Good times. My mantra throughout that painful process was "I only have to do this once." I repeated this to myself a lot during that time...and I suggest you do the same when you get frustrated as you're getting started!

Insurance Agent

As with any professional on your team, good customer service is a vital quality to find in your insurance agent. You'll need to make sure they get the full picture of what needs to be covered as it relates to both your business and your life. Your insurance needs will drastically change once you become a business owner, and your agent needs to evaluate all aspects of those changes. This is no longer something you can shop around for the cheapest price like you can for car insurance, for example.

Payroll Provider

If you are going to have any payroll needs, I am pretty adamant when it comes to suggesting a payroll provider verses doing it on your own or having your CPA do it.

First, payroll is messy. There are several different agencies involved, each agency has different due dates, tax rates, etc., and all filings with those agencies have to coincide. It's very easy to mess one thing up and create a snowball effect of problems.

Second, payroll agencies generally aren't kind with payroll penalties. Some of the payroll remittances you are making aren't really your money. It's your employees' money you're withholding from their paycheck and remitting on their behalf. For that reason, penalties can be steep and add up quickly.

Third, most payroll providers are very inexpensive. The benefits of the services they provide absolutely out-weigh the minimal cost. All it would take is a few payments being made late throughout the year to spend more on tax penalties than paying an expert to take care of it for you.

Fourth, it adds efficiency to your business. The provider pays your employees and does all the tax filings for you. You can rest assured it's all being done correctly without taking up insane amounts of your time.

While my firm is capable of doing payroll, it is not our focus. We cannot provide some of the benefits a payroll provider can, and I want my clients to have the best service possible for all aspects of their businesses. I would question a CPA firm wanting to take on payroll. We refer all new clients to Automated Payroll Services located in Lafayette, IN. It is a local firm with nation-wide experience which provides customer service well above even the nationally known payroll providers I've dealt with. I have had several cases where surprise fees and a lack of customer service from other providers has ended up very detrimental and costly to the customer. Not only does APS provide outstanding and inexpensive services, but its customer service ensures you are taken care of properly and efficiently.

Marketing Professionals

Surprisingly, "if you build it, they might not come." Attracting your ideal customers/clients is going to take work and it's easy to make costly mistakes here.

The first thing you'll need is a good brand image including a logo and business cards. You don't need to spend a lot of money here at first, but if you have it in your budget to hire a designer to lay the minimal foundation of a proper logo/card, please do that rather than create your own.

Next you'll want to invest some time and thought into who you want to attract and the most effective ways to do it. Some marketing strategies are better for people who have more time than money. Others are better for people with more money than time. (Note: Be careful about going to anyone who sells ad space as your initial marketing advisor.) Do your own research to become educated on the best marketing strategies for your business and you'll save yourself money and hours of frustration.

IT Expert

Whether you're going to be a small or large business, you will have at least one computer. (If you're considering not using a computer at all with your business...well...um...you might not succeed.) You definitely should consult with an information technology (IT) expert to make sure you have the right equipment (and that it's well protected). That support could be vital if/when you have computer issues. Computer downtime does nothing but take away from efficiency.

Chapter 5

Accounting FUN!

Accounting Systems

Well, bad news. Whether you like it or not, you have to figure out an accounting system and get organized. You have options. You can use a manual system, computer software, or outsource this service.

In order for a manual system to make sense, you would need to have a very low amount of volume in regard to transactions, few receivables to track, and probably no employees. By "manual system" I mean you would only use paper to track your income and expenses. For example, you could use a basic bank account check register to record each transaction. However, it doesn't take much activity for a computer system to be worth it.

I recommend the most common computer software package: QuickBooks™, and there are reasons it's as popular as it is. It is user-friendly, you can make it as simple or as complex as you want, and it works. Once you get the hang of it, you can be very efficient while always knowing the monetary aspects of your business including how much cash you have, who owes you money, and, most importantly, where your business is profitable. The more information you have, the better decisions you'll be able to make.

I like QuickBooks™. First, I have yet to come across a QB file I couldn't fix. What this means to you is you can do the best you can and as long as you follow a few basic rules (I'll get into that, later) without fear you're doing something irreversibly wrong.

Second, I love the "class" feature. Classes allow you to track your income and expenses and run reports by groups which are set up the way it makes the most sense for your business.

For example, I've set up my accounting firm's employees as classes. This allows me to run profit and loss reports by employee and see the profitability of each person. With that information, I can make good decisions, such as recognizing when an employee deserves a raise and bonus or determining services needing cost adjustments. Classes are an easy way to add value to your accounting information.

The third option for your accounting system is to outsource the function completely or partially. Complete outsourcing is best for businesses in industries that collect payment before or at the time services are rendered, (e.g., restaurants, retail stores, or contractors who deliver invoices upon job completion).

When figuring out what system is best for your business, there are a few additional factors to consider. Does your industry have software available to specifically address other business processes in addition to accounting functions? How computer literate is the accountant in your company? If you, the business owner, will perform the accounting, is this the best use of your time? Does a bank or other relationship require certain levels of accounting and assurance?

Getting Organized

No matter what accounting system you use, there are a few basic rules that, if followed, will make accounting less painful and more efficient, allow you to have the information about your business you need readily available, and keep your accounting and tax fees as low as possible.

Rule #1 – As early as possible, open a bank account for the business and do not co-mingle personal and business funds.

Rule #2 - File all paperwork alphabetically. Here is a common mistake I see people make: they start their business in June, label a file "June," and start putting all customer invoices, vendor receipts and other paper work for June in that folder. However, this filing system is not very useful at all. Instead, start a file for each customer, each vendor and each employee. When you need paperwork, you know where to find it.

Rule #3 – Add a good description with every transaction you record. If you are using a paper check register or QuickBooks™, every transaction should be noted with the check number, date, amount, who it was to/from and a description of the transaction.

If you are using QuickBooks™ or other software, put that same information in your system. With QuickBooks™, it is virtually impossible to screw it up so badly I can't figure it out and fix it. As long as you have recorded the transactions and put enough information to tell me about each, I can adjust properly when necessary. This also helps if you have an out-of-the-ordinary transaction. Rather than wondering where to post it, place it in an account called "Ask My Accountant" and add a good description. You can keep moving forward while alerting both of us there is a transaction to address when we're able.

Accounting Fees and Tax Filing Requirements

Hopefully you've already done (or plan to do) a budget and projection to show your business can be profitable. Sometimes it's hard to do this accurately when you don't know your expenses. This is especially true with all the initial costs you'll face in the first year during set up. On top of that, it's hard to get a handle on all of the various filing requirements and when they're due. The following are just a few of the common filing requirements along with common estimates for accounting fees in 2013. *Please note this list is not all-encompassing and accounting fees listed are estimates based on my average client size:*

Common Filing Requirements & Fees

Description	Due Date	Accounting Fees
Monthly/Quarterly Bookkeeping (if outsourced)	N/A	$150-$500
Annual Entity Income Tax Return	March 15/ April 15	$550-$950
Annual Form 1099s	January 31	$150-$300
Annual Property Tax Return	May 15	$150-$300

Tressa Heath, CPA

Chapter 6

Don't Let the Tax Tail Wag the Dog

Yes, this is one of those many lame sayings my accounting colleagues have come up with.

I've seen business owners lose sight of why they want to pay low taxes. The reason is to end up with more money for both the short- and long-term. It is not simply to pay the government as little as possible. A tax deduction is only worth the tax it saves.

Here are some examples of misguided questions and thought processes...

Wrong: Should I buy a big piece of equipment so I can get a tax deduction?

Well, I don't know...do you need a big piece of equipment? If not and you just want the tax deduction, I'll gladly send you a bill for $20,000. My fees are also tax deductions.

Just Silly: My insurance agent said I can lower my insurance costs, but I don't want to lose the deduction.

Hopefully it's obvious why this is wrong. Think of it in the inverse: Would you turn down a raise purely because you will have to pay taxes on the increased salary? I hope not! If you can relate to this thought process, you're not alone, but hopefully this chapter is hitting home and changing the way you think and make financial decisions.

Nope: It's my first year of business. I'm supposed to be able to show a loss. How can you help me do this?

Hello?! It's a good thing to not be one of those statistics! I had a client say this to me almost word for word several years ago. He was the only one in his household working, had been laid off and ended up going into business for himself in a similar field out of desperation to provide for his family. This business was very profitable without having to take out any loans from the bank. It was a pure cash business. How the heck could he be operating at a taxable loss? It's not a rule you must have a loss in your first year, and there's no magic accounting wand to wave to make it so.

Right: I need to buy a big piece of equipment. Should I buy it before or after year end?

Now we're on the right track. You are going to make this investment, which we can now assume is a necessary one, but it's close to year end. We need to talk strategy in terms of which year the deduction might be worth more to you.

I'm not saying paying taxes is awesome…but profitability is awesome and taxes are just part of that. Of course, there are ways and strategies to lower taxes and that's where the conversation should remain with your accountant. Tax strategy is about paying as few taxes as possible over time rather than in any one year. Part of the goal is accomplishing deductions that pay you rather than a vendor, such as paying a family member for services or making deductible contributions to your retirement plan.

Part of the strategy is *not* to have unnecessary expenses and operate at a loss! In fact, depending on the tax environment and other factors, you may want to push expenses into the following year and report as much income as possible in the current year. If this sounds crazy or confusing, we should talk soon about your specific situation.

Tressa Heath, CPA

Chapter 7

Communicate Frequently with Your CPA...
No Matter How Painful it Is!

Okay, okay. You're almost done reading this book about accounting.

Really and truly though, communication with your accountant and other members of your professional "posse" is very important. This doesn't mean you have to call them every day. However, hopefully you've found people you can communicate with well. Utilize their knowledge. That's why they're there! Don't hesitate to check in with them periodically. Definitely run any big financial assessments past them before the decision is made, and think about having them look at your books a couple of times a year to make sure you're not missing something. As I said in an earlier chapter, it's much healthier to be proactive rather than reactive.

I want my clients to reach out to me when necessary no matter how big or small the issue! For this reason, my billing clock doesn't start ticking when I pick up the phone or open an email. Accounting is too important to your business and I don't want any barriers to be in the way of your communicating with me.

Wrap it Up, Lady

I get asked *a lot* how I could possibly do what I do. I do this because I love it! It's interesting to hear about each client's story and be a part of the success in each business.

I'd love to hear about you and your business! You can visit us on our website at www.heath-cpa.com or email me directly to tressa@heath-cpa.com Tell me about yourself as well as ask any follow up questions or request clarity on something I didn't cover in this book. You can also register for my (not annoying I promise) newsletter mailing list to stay current on tax topics and get info about the various FREE QuickBooks™ and tax workshops I hold.

I hope you've learned a little bit by reading this book and put it down a smarter and more confident entrepreneur.

Now, go make some money!

Tressa Heath, CPA

About Tressa

Tressa Heath is a CPA, QuickBooks ProAdvisor, wife, and mother of three. She has (unofficially) been deemed "Lafayette's Coolest CPA" by her clients for her fun-loving personality and authentic communication style.

Tressa is a Lafayette, Indiana native, a graduate of Central Catholic and Indiana University – Purdue University Indianapolis (IUPUI), and heavily involved in her community. You'll find her serving on several nonprofit boards including Matrix Pregnancy Center, Big Brothers Big Sisters of Greater Lafayette, and Greater Lafayette Commerce Chamber Council. After years of working in various firms gaining extensive experience in tax and accounting, she launched her own accounting firm, Heath CPA and Associates, in December of 2011.

Visit **www.heath-cpa.com** to discover how Tressa and her team can help with your business needs, or to check the schedule for her QuickBooks™ seminars.